From across an ocean to the shores of Cornwall via a career in the Royal Navy; now retired, this man (and his dog) has journeyed through life and love, with much laughter and many interests and experiences along the way. All of which have shaped memories, thoughts and opinions that are now shared to make you think, smile and perhaps relate to.

Please read slowly and gather your thoughts as life is a journey not a race.

Poetry is a wonderful thing
by Lowen Pengoose ©Nov19

Poetry is a wonderful thing
It can make you dance, it can make you sing

Think of someone, let your mind fly
Let the words flow, and don't wonder why

People may scoff, people may scorn
But they haven't walked, In those boots that you've worn

The places you've been, the things you have seen
Would make some men wonder, and make others scream

But never despair, always look up
Never go backwards , the future's in front

Life is a gift, a precious one too,
Not to be squandered, but loved through and through

Some may be lengthy, others not so
So laugh when you can, and play in the snow

When the race is run, and it's time to depart
Say thanks to poetry, for playing its part

1

By Lowen Pengoose ©April 2020

In the beginning of time, there was only one number,
And that number, (you guessed it) was 1,
No other numbers, existed back then,
so nobody did any sums,

Matey, said, here , if I have number 1,
What do I call it then, when it's gone?
So he sat and he thought, and he thought, and he sat!
And exclaimed "It's called - Not 1"

So this guy decided, 'Not 1' wasn't right
He needed a new name, for 'Not 1',
"The answer is simple, I'll just lose the 'T'"
Which is how 'Not 1' became 'None'

Oh, he was so happy, (Larry was his name)
He didn't know quite what to do,
Whilst playing around he finally found - another,
So now he had 2!

Well, with a 2 and a 1, (and don't forget none)
It all became clear, do you see?
Larry did his first sum, put the 2 with the 1
And that's when the world first saw 3

3 was so happy to have entered this way
But Larry was feeling perplexed
Having a 3 and a 2 and a 1 (don't forget none)
He didn't know quite what came next

Did he look for another? or just keep these four?
The world waited on Larry's next action
He thought four's enough, so he took back the 1,
And swiftly created subtraction

There was no looking back now, onward and up
Larry was keeping the sum alive
Along came the 4, and whilst looking for more
Quickly saw the arrival of 5

As quick as you like, 6 popped her head out
He couldn't stop 7 nor 8?
But 9 was the last, for quite a long while,
Larry was happy again, ...just to wait

The whole world was waiting to see what transpired
There was silence, and quiet.......and then!
With a shout and a scream, and a dance inbetween!
Larry proclaimed ! ..."I now have a 10!"

How did this happen, what did you do?
We thought all the numbers were done
Larry smiled a wry smile, and winked and he said,
"I just put my first 1, with None"

Have A Word

By Lowen Pengoose ©Nov19

I love to read a dictionary
I don't mean end to end,
I dip in every now and then,
like chatting with a friend

I'll pick a word at random
I'll flick the page, then stop!
Place my digit upon the page
And read the word atop

Perhaps a verb, a clause or noun
Will have something to say
It matters not I'm keen to learn
A new word every day

Some are short, some are long
Some lie in between
The syllables don't matter
It's understanding what they mean

To comprehend, to understand
That really is the key
To life's enriching process
That learning words can be

To have, the expertise and art
Of picking words at will
And using them unexpectedly
Is really quite the thrill

It can make you seem quite clever
But be careful, you're forewarned
Using words you're not sure of
Just shows you're misinformed

Now don't start me on commas
Semi colons are nobody's friend
And Gratuitous use of apostrophes
Where will it ever end?

Punctuation's a different matter
Where will the full stop land?
Depending if you want to finish.
Your sentence.
As planned

Alternate Title
by Lowen Pengoose ©2020

You Ain't Seen Nothin' Yet,
No Matter What, Never Forget,
Thinking Out Loud, No Surrender,
Please Be With Me,
Love me Tender.

Take a Walk on the Wild Side,
Travelling Light, Ticket to Ride,
All Over the World, I Walk the Line,
Go Your Own Way,
Time after Time.

Do Anything you Wanna Do,
Run for Home, Into the Blue,
Many Rivers to Cross, Stay with Me,
Don't Look Back in Anger,
Blowin' Free.

When a Blind Man Cries,
Don't Shed a Tear, Behind Blue Eyes,
I Can See Clearly Now, Come As You Are,
You've Got a Friend,
Whiskey in the Jar.

Stuck in the Middle With You,
Happy Together, Who Knew,
Love is All Around, Perfect Day,
Love of my Life,
Half the World Away.

The Whole of the Moon,
My Sweet Lord, See You Soon,
It Must be Love, Here Comes the Sun,
Have a Nice Day,
Born to Run.

My Ever Changing Moods,
American Pie, All the Young Dudes,
More Than a Feeling, Horse with No Name,
Need You Now,
Virginia Plain.

Knockin' on Heavens's Door,
Radar Love, Blood on the Dance Floor,
With or Without You, End of the Line,
The Power of Love,
Sweet Child O'Mine.

(Sittin' On) the Dock of the Bay,
Alright Now, What a Beautiful Day,
Waterloo Sunset, Sex is on Fire,
Because the Night,
Higher and Higher.

Another One Bites the Dust,
After the Goldrush, Diamonds and Rust,
Suspicious Minds, For What it's Worth,
Turn to Stone,
Planet Earth.

The Final Countdown, 54321,
Down Down, We've Only Just Begun,
Maybe Tomorrow, Yesterday,
I Can See for Miles,
See Emily Play.

Stairway to Heaven, Highway to Hell,
A Different Corner, Wishing Well,
Heroes, Wonderful Tonight,
Angels,
Ships in the Night.

Stand and Deliver, Fight for your Right,
Crazy Horses, Tonight's the Night,
Come as you are, Go your Own Way,
Hollywood Nights,
Maggie May.

Alright Now, Someone Like You,
American Girl, A Boy Named Sue,
A New Kid in Town, Going Underground,
Spanish Train,
.......Homeward Bound!

Chocolate and Cake

By Lowen Pengoose ©26th April 2020

How can I be
A better me
Vitamin D
Or Vitamin Sea?

The beach and sand
And holding hands
Is all it takes
And chocolate..and cakes!

It's all in the mind
We must be kind
To see the good
The trees from the wood

For me to improve
I will have to remove
Those blocks in the road
Increasing my load

For when I am free
Of what burdens me
I can excel
Released from my hell

And then you will see
A much better me
My heart won't ache
I have chocolate....and cake!

Tide Times

By Lowen Pengoose ©4 Sep 2020

Time and tide wait for no-one
So the proverb goes
One marches steadily onward
The other ebbs and flows

Both have their very own cycle
The tide controlled by the moon
They rise and fall twice a day
'Le cycle de la lune'

Time differs, it only moves forward
Never backward or stopping still
It counts in minutes and seconds
Have you got time to kill?

As time moves on, tides rise and fall
We live our lives in hope
When tides are low we disappear
Struggling to cope

Tides go out and come back in
A metaphor for life?
Some days are good and some are bad
Harmony versus strife

Our personal clocks are ticking
Don't hesitate, 'Seize the Day'
Our personal tides will come and go
Make sure you have your say

Give good advice whenever asked
Be quick to pass it on
This becomes your tidal flow
When the tide is out, it's gone

If help is ever needed
Be sure to ask for it
Someone else's clock will strike
And you will benefit

These checks and balances all work out
The circle of life never ends
Help each other when on the ebb
Is the message we should send

The ship in the harbour cannot sail
Until the tide is high
When the time is right, we cast off
With a calm wind and blue sky

My last high tide, now on the turn
My clock ticks its final seconds
I've come and gone, as do the tides
Eternity now beckons

My personal timepiece standing still
No more beating heart
Or happiness or sadness
No need for a tidal chart

The Artist's Lament

By Lowen Pengoose ©Aug 27 2020

I'd love to paint my little house
Which stands beside the sea
It's english country garden
And pear and apple tree

I told her of my grand design
A smile came on her face
"I'll go and tidy up inside
To smarten up the place"

This seemed a little strange to me
What difference would that make?
My thoughts were on my work of art
A portrait, maybe landscape?

Men and womens minds diverge
"I know" I hear you say
"I've ordered all the paint you need"
From that online shop, eBay

"I also called those lovely boys
With boards and scaffold poles"
They'll be here by tomorrow
So you can start to fill the holes

I donned my bib'n'braces
With more than a little sweat
Climbed aloft the structure
Without a safety net

The wind was gently blowing
As I held on for dear life
I just wanted to paint a picture
To give my darling wife

I thought it best to start afresh
Painting all that I could see
I painted almost all the house
And most of the apple tree

Thinking I had finished my task
And suffered for my art
Those immortal words rang in my ears
"I've got some new colour charts"

This revelation was a shock
Like a cannon's mighty BOOM!
Deep joy of joys, my lucky day
I'm painting the living room

Silk, Matt or Emulsion
Laquer must be applied
Apple blossom, arctic blue
These colours that I've tried

The skirting boards are sanded down
The walls are sugar soaped
The ceilings need an undercoat
Abandon ye all hope

Undercoat, or overcoat,
Roller, pad or brush
Decisions so important
Take it slowly, dare not rush

Now I'm finished, over and done
I've washed and cleaned me gear,
I'll not get caught like that again
I think It's time for beer

My fate was well and truly sealed
I would get to paint my house
Not the way I had in mind
Thanks to my lovely spouse

The 'Silk Road' Clay Trail
By Lowen Pengoose ©2020

I exited left onto Eastcliffe Road
Headed due south, following the Highway Code
Took the footpath, down by the shop
When I reached the sea, I had to stop
Turned to starboard, walked down the beach
Until Par Harbour, I surely reached
Ambled around the harbour wall
Minding each step, careful not to fall
Across the footbridge, when I came to it
A half mile further, to the beach named 'Spit'
Then looked across, o'er Carlyon Bay
To Charlestown harbour, whence they shipped China clay

This industry alas, now in decline
Once warranted it's very own railway line
Transporting 'White Gold' from Clay Country
Down to the coast then globally, by sea
William Cookworthy knew this was his gold,
The China Clay story, about to unfold
Tregonning Hill, where it all began
Where Cookworthy hatched his master plan
To make porcelain, as fine as Chinese
European markets available for taking at ease
The prize he sought, known as 'Moorstone'
It ran through the county, the Cornish backbone

From Charlestown head north, to Clay Country
The scars from mining so plain to see
Up through St. Dennis, Foxhole and Carthew
Discovering the trail, as many folk do
Understanding the hardships the villagers faced
In pursuit of the fortunes that everyone chased
The motto of Cornwall is 'One and All'
For the riches of china clay, they answered the call
Over two hundred years, white gold would provide
and the success it brought, bred true Cornish pride
Who would have thought this dust from the ground
Was more valuable than gold, if it could be found

Finer than talcum, but exceedingly rare
It was there for the taking, if anyone dare
Dare he did and the die was cast
Unbeknownst to him, the seam so vast
65,000 tonnes, each year from the earth
7,000 workers, each proving their worth
At great expense, water pumped hard and fast
To split clay from granite, in open cast
The rivers ran white, down St. Austell bay
Manufacturing thrived, it was here to stay
Bal maidens toiled, working clay as it dried
To be shipped round the world, on the next high tide

Villages grew, North, South, East and West
Cornish clay was regarded as simply the best
Two hundred and fifty years or more
Saw the wealth of Cornwall continue to soar
This magical kaolin, in such great demand
Creating 'Sky Tips' from waste rock and sand
These would create a unique skyline
Which will define the process for all of time
But each ton of clay produced eight of waste
And this growing problem could not be erased
As a solution was sought, fate lent a hand
By deciding enough had been torn from this land...

...A lode in Brazil, second to none
The decline of Cornwall had surely begun
Easier to extract, with cheap labour cost
The 'White Gold' of Kernow was steadily lost
Cornish Alps and white rivers, the county was hushed
The lifeblood of Cornwall now totally crushed
'Twas the end of an era, no one could deny
For Cornish china clay, folk lived, worked and died
Now villages sleep and foundries lay dormant
China clay extraction, no longer important
Hensbarrow Moors, the only mine left
The production, towns and workers bereft

I walk the Clay Country, now known for it's 'Trails'
Our walks and cycleways, regaling their tales
Of mining heritage, in days of yore
China Clay, Copper, Tin, and so much more
I walk from Luxulyan, Trethurgy, Carclaze
Past Eden Project, and imagine those days
Onward to Ponts Mill, through St. Blazey Gate
Picture the scene, when Cornwall was great
Nearly complete on my tour of our past
I invite you dear reader, to compare and contrast
A circular walk, back on Eastcliffe Road
I'll turn left and return, to my Cornish abode

Pirates

By Lowen Pengoose ©June 10 2020

"Shiver me Timbers", said the Pirate,
For that is how he talks,
Bangin' his wooden leg on deck,
For that is how he walks.

Parrot on his shoulder,
Patch across his eye,
Crew atop t'gallants,
Jolly Roger flying high.

Crew of ragamuffins,
Some boys, and some old hands,
Sailing o'er the oceans,
To foreign, far off lands.

So If they spies a Frenchy,
And feeling somewhat bold,
They'll come about and broadside her,
And plunder them for gold.

Then they sits in shallow waters,
Behind headlands, up a cove,
And sail in fast and furious,
To relieve your treasure trove.

Blackbeard was most famous,
Edward Teach, his real name,
His reputation preceded him,
As he gathered fortune and fame.

Anne Bonny too, was a Pirate,
Born in Cork, in a tumble down shack,
moving to Nassau, Bahamas,
As the wife of Calico Jack

When becalmed at sea, as happens
Pirates drink grog, and dance a jig
But man your station when drunken
And say hello to the brig

Worse punishments, they were aplenty
If you failed to hoist the sails
When the Bosun piped the order
Ensured the cat o'ninetails

Now Privateers, were not Pirates
'Letters of Marque' allowed their deeds
Approved by our country's government
To further their nefarious needs

They attacked foreign shipping in wartime
To seize bounty, crew and craft
Being sold on under 'Prize Law', for cash
Hands muster for payment, abaft

If your lookout, in the crow's nest above
Shouts "Pirates Off the Starboard Bow"
Ensure your Skipper turns hard about
Retreat as fast as the winds allow

For those Pirates are quick and sneaky
And this will come as no shocker,
If you meet them Pirates, face to face
You'll end up in Davy Jones' Locker

Patsy, My Wife, My World
By Lowen Pengoose ©April 2020

You're heaven not hell
You know me so well
You're everything to me

You're love, not hate
You're my bestest mate
You're everything to me

You're my up, not down
You're my round and round
You're everything to me

You're land, you're sea
You'll always be
Everything to me

You're black you're white
You're out of sight
You're everything to me

You're in you're out
You whisper, don't shout
You're everything to me

You're everything to me my love
Everything to me
And everything I have in life
I owe it all to thee

I cry a tear to you my dear
You're everything to me
I don't deserve an ounce of you
Why do you love me, dear

Lady of Par

By Lowen Pengoose ©28/11/2019

She stands between, the sea and land
Awaiting me, to take her hand
I sometimes do, I sometimes don't
I mostly can, I rarely won't

I love her look, her changing moods
Sometimes she shouts, sometimes she broods,
No matter what, she's always true
And ev'ry day, she starts anew

She loves my dog, he loves her back
The gift of fun, the lively crack (craic)
Whate'er the time, whate'er the day
I know that she, is here to stay

I stand so close, To smell her scent
I can't resist, it's time I went
To see her face, what mood today,
To maybe walk?, or maybe play?

No matter what, I do not care
I always love , when I am there
A special place, I'll always reach
When I walk upon, My own Par Beach

Is It?
By Lowen Pengoose ©April 25th 2020

Is it me?
Is it you?
Is it us?
Is it true?

Can we go?
Should we not?
Let me know
If you cannot

We can run
Or we can stay
Have some fun?
Or fly away?

Does HE know?
SHE does not
My heart's aglow
Yours, maybe not?

I know for sure
I know you, too
Your heart is pure
I do love you

So how do we
Go from here?
If I can see
The way is clear

Shall we escape?
And run away
Or face them both
And seize the day?

I'd rather run
Than face a fight
When all things done
Our future's bright

You are my friend
And that's a fact
You'll never bend
I've got your back

We'll live a life
Pure and true
You'll be my wife
I do love you xx

We Never Saw the Cliché Coming
By Lowen Pengoose ©29th April 2020

We never saw it coming
Said the ostrich, head in sand
It certainly isn't our problem
It's contained in a far off land

If Ignorance is bliss, they say
We must be in paradise
Better safe than sorry
Or we may just pay the price

It's an uphill battle
Social distancing is a start
Actions speak louder than words
We all must play our part

Keep a stiff upper lip and your eye on the ball
Any lies that we tell will only be small

There's no time like the present
The science must be followed
We're all in this together
And jobs they must be furloughed

You certainly can't please everyone
Frontline staff for sure
Not enough PPE?
A million pieces more?

So, In the very nick of time
We locked each other down,
We isolated and shielded
And rarely went to town

To protect the vulnerable, weak and young
Don't spread fake news, please hold your tongue

Please give me a ballpark figure
Will it be 6 weeks 8, or 10?
We're not quite out of the woods yet mate
Government will tell you when

I heard it through the grapevine
The lockdown's being released
It's all about the timing
We musn't feed the beast

What doesn't kill you, makes you stronger
Is a phrase you often hear
Tell that to the 40,000 plus
For whom we shed a tear

When all of this is over and maybe it's not too late
We can all refocus and start over again
with a brand new wiped clean slate

Ode 2 - 19 Covid
Pronounced "Ode to Covid-19"
By Lowen Pengoose ©March 2020

Hot Town..
Summertime..
In lockdown...

How are you..?
Going to get through..?
Are you running..?
Out of things do..?

Easy for me..?
My dwelling place..
Numbers 3..

Big garden..?
At 'Chez Pog'..
Me and 'er..
And the dog..

No fun..?
If your..
Number is 1..

Daily update..?
On your own..?
Simple tasks..
Whinge and moan..

Lie in again..?
Sleepless..?
Up by 10..?

Every day..?
Therapy..?
Walk the pooch..
Down to the sea..

Groundhog Day..
49..
No more to say..

Radio off..
Same old tunes..
Saving grace..?
Walking the dunes..

Good News..
Return to work..?
If you choose..

Safety first..?
Bosses swear..
2 metres apart..
"Because we care"..?

Schools next..?
Teachers do..
your safety checks..

No exams..?
What a waste..
Repent at leisure..
Act in haste..

Unlimited..
Exercise..
Exhibited..

Parks open..?
Visit friends..?
Second spike..?
The end.

Time and Emotion Study

By Lowen Pengoose ©20th May 2020

Going through the motions
The world revolves at speed
Waking up and sleeping
Performing when we need

Going through emotions
The world spins slowly round
Love and hate, and tears and fears
Showing smiles, but wearing frowns

Enduring disbelief and doubt
The hands of time will spin
Never knowing where it all began
Or the ending will begin

We're heading to extinction
Time flies while standing still
Washing hands and cars and clothes and things
Waking only to take our sleeping pill

The treadmill of life is increasing its pace
While we're running on the spot
We're giving our all and coming up short
You have to give more than you've got

A Lidl ode

By Lowen Pengoose ©9th April 2020

(Written during the first lockdown whilst queuing outside Lidl to shop for essentials)

Like soldiers and dominoes
We all stand in line
Waiting quite orderly
Until it is time

To get, our basic daily needs
Just to buy a crust
We do this for each other
For each other we must trust

So what is deemed essential?
Is it bread or is it flour
What do you deem most important
In this, our darkest hour

I would say our friendship
I would even venture love
These I value more than food
These are way above

But eat we must and shop we will
This will soon be at an end
Then we will tell our stories,
Laugh, and be together once again.

The rhythm of life is changing
We need more beats of the drum
More dancing and singing and laughing required
Yet we barely manage to hum

Nature has her own cycle
Like clocks, the moon and tide
Progressing at a pace all her own
A frequency she decides

So, when you hear of a happening
Tsunami, famine or war
Think to yourself, man made or no?
Nature just evening the score?

When the Earth is fed up crying
Allowing life to stay
She has to do something drastic
Ctrl-Alt-Del in her own way

She tried it once, a long time ago
With a horror, beyond belief
mankind didn't listen and change its ways
Despite the massive grief

Humanity would not listen,
Their future, all sunny and green
Nature tried, just one more time
Wreaking havoc with Covid-19

Your password to Freedom is 06061944

By Lowen Pengoose ©06/06/2020

6th June 1944

...D-Day,
..the landing,
..that saw,

The beginning of...
..the ending of,
..the war

The beaches soft...
..the shells,
..and men,
..so hard

Youngsters all,
..many will fall..
..human life,
..too easy,
..To discard

A forward push..
..misunderstood,
..no retreat,
..no one would

Onward now..
..one and all,
..United we stand..
..divided,
..We fall

Onward now..
..to Victory,
..Honour bound,
..to set them..
..FREE!

Glory is..
..not what
I seek,
Why could man
..Not turn,
..the other cheek?

I cannot describe..
..the horror,
I saw

Thank God,
..after this
There will be..
..no more
...war

Victorious England
By Lowen Pengoose ©2020

Two little letters V and E
Why do they mean so much to me

For those that gave us everything
So we can laugh, and dance and sing

Their sacrifice we will not know
they have enabled our lives to grow

They fought for us though we were not born
From heroes cloth they were surely torn

Asking for nothing, They gave their all
So that we can walk so proud and tall

The need was great., they did not flinch
The going was tough, they gave not one inch

When it was over and peace declared
We hailed the heroes who were never scared

Scared they were, but always true
Fighting for themselves, ...and me, ...and you

Letters make words, and words make sense
Bravely they fought, in our defence

So when you think of the alphabet
Perhaps you'll remember, and never forget

We owe these men of land, air and sea
So I remember you all, with the letters V and E

This Flight Tonight
(Battle of Taranto, 11-12th November 1940)
By Lowen Pengoose 7th July 2020
With thanks to Sid Oates

Ahoy there, me lasses, me hearties, me lads,
To see you all here in rig, mufty, and rags
Pull up a bollard, let me tell you a story
Of when I joined up, not for fame or for glory
I'd entered this world back in twenty-four,
By age of fifteen, I was fighting a war

"You're too young to join" the recruiting Chief barked,
So I changed my birthdate on the form, duly marked
Boy Seaman first class William H. Davis, Sir!
The rest of my training went by in a blur
Then climbing the gangway, trepid thoughts in my head
My ship was preparing to set sail for the med

Mediterranean Sea, make way with best speed,
Further orders to follow, "Yes Sir" indeed
Now I sit here recounting, to tell you my tale
In the lounge of the Legion, with a cold pint of ale
I remind you young sailors, that I took no delight,
In the events that occurred on that black, fateful night,

Unbeknownst to us all, history was to be made,
With a daring and dangerous and dauntless air raid
On that cold winter night, in the month of November,
Admiral Cunningham in charge, I so clearly remember,
Operation Judgement, I recall the name
"Regia Marina's" First Squadron, was always the aim

'Illustrious' the carrier, on that cold winters' night
That provided the platform, for the Swordfishes flight
So listen up now, young fella me lad
Let me tell you the story of the battle we had
As a young jack tar sailor, still learning the ropes,
Working the deck with high dreams, and high hopes

Twenty one aircraft, at sea and at war
Preparing to strike at the enemy's core
The order to go was eagerly awaited
But this operation was desperately fated
Originally planned for Trafalgar day
An aircraft on fire, forced 'The Fleet' to delay

"Eagle" was chosen, she would now be the lead
Her fuel tanks were leaking, so she had to leave
We thought the delay would prevent the attack
Rumours were rife; we would have to turn back
The Admirals conversed and altered their plan
Which would fall on the shoulders of just one man

Rear Admiral Lyster, he took control
He developed the strategy, to deliver the goal
Now I'll mention it here, as I finish my drink
On that night in question, there was no time to think
The aircraft were ranged and fuelled for their flight
None of us knew, if they would make it that night

So we prayed for good weather, and god speed their souls
Pilots so young at their aircraft's controls
I was so young, and so were they,
The ultimate price, we were willing to pay
But we were a team all wanting to fight
Because this was- 'That Flight Tonight '

From the southwest they came, flying in low
The 'Conte di Cavour' took a fateful blow
Before she was lost, all her guns took aim
Fired at the Swordfish and downed the bi-plane
The attacks were relentless, until early morn
But hits on 'Littorio' left Italians forlorn

'Caio Duilio', was lost in that raid
Half of the fleet, was the price that they paid
As we sit round the table you young'uns and me
Pray tell what drew you, to a life on the sea?
For me it was always the carriers I craved
And airplanes, like models, as a boy, that I made

To see them fly high, in skies so blue
Cavaliers of the air, so dashing and true
Then higher still, near out of sight
Engines a'roaring, with the gift of flight
I was just a young lad, maybe eight years or nine
All that I wanted for this young life of mine

My 'Old Man' was a Sailor, when I was born
Sailed the West Indies, and round Cape Horn
When the world went to war, he went Merchant to Royal
My Dad was the bravest man, steadfast and loyal
So I've always had this love for the sea
A sailors life, was destined for me

To combine my two loves, the sea and the air
Would be quite simple, causing no despair
Joining 'The Andrew', where was the harm?
To operate the aircraft of the Fleet Air Arm
So we have lots in common, you youngsters and me
A love for adventure, aircraft and sea

Now back to my story, the first wave complete
Ensuring the loss of most of their fleet
Dodging barrage balloons and 800 guns
The second wave started their midnight run
They were only 8 strong, 5 torpedoes, 3 bombs
Did their duty that night, without sweaty palms

At the conclusion of the deadly attack
The first wave returned, not all made it back
For the next ninety minutes, 'Illustrious' drew breath
Could the second wave make it, and all cheat death?
The price we paid upon that day, I recall with a mighty sigh
Two Fairey Swordfish aircraft less, shot down from the sky

Two aircrew they were captured, prisoners of war
Two brave souls were also lost, to sadly fly no more
Events that night fill me with fear
But also with pride, that I hold dear
I fought with loyalty for the rest of the war
Somehow surviving five years more
Losing good shipmates, family and friends
In a war that seemed, would never end

Eleven November Nineteen Forty
The Fleet Air Arm endentured their story
The first in the world, carrier air raid
Not ever knowing, the history they made
The Fleet Air Arm, on that day takes a toast
And praise the brave airmen, but never a boast

For we know in our hearts, history was made
On that night in November, by those so brave
So it falls upon us, to remember that night
And remember those that were lost in the fight
Forever remembered, never forgotten,
All those heroes, living and fallen

We readied ourselves on the wintery deck
Aircraft ranged, - 'before flight' checked
Whilst waiting to strike, intelligence grew
So the striking force could fly straight through
Barrage balloons, countless enemy guns
Dodged torpedo nets, and adjusted their runs

To ensure that what they did that night
Would forever enshrine the Fleet Air Arm's might
The intelligence showed, without any doubt
The Italian fleet would be surely caught out
The 'Fleet in Being' is all well and fine
Until it comes to the reckoning time

If you're not prepared to sail and fight
You'll succumb to the force of the Fleet Air Arm's might
I remember it well, just like yesterday
We worked through the night, no time to pray
The aircraft must fly, fix them when broken
The engines so noisy, no words were spoken

Torpedoes were loaded, the flight deck steady
Those Swordfish aircraft were battle ready
Williamson RN, led the first wave of twelve,
All thoughts on the sortie, none for themselves,
Nine more followed, one had to return
Auxiliary tank leak, no fuel to burn

Taxiing at night, a collision the result
Thankfully no injury, to add to insult
Successfully launched, after a swift repair,
20 minutes were lost as he took to the air
Armed only with flares, torpedoes and bombs
Their targets were sighted at harbour 'Mar Grande'

Bayley and Slaughter you gave your all
Williamson and Scarlett, prisoners of war
To all my shipmates, living and gone
I live with your memories, you'll forever live on
Brothers in Arms a hell that we shared
We fought together because we all cared

I continued to serve, until seventy nine
Rising up through the ranks, during my time
Saw the arrival of jets, and the steam catapult
Fought in more wars, yet none were my fault
I look back on my life, and am proud to say
I would not have wanted it, any other way

Now I sit here and thank you, for indulging my tales
I have a chest full of medals and you've bought me my ales
But you are the future, our country's best
You carry the mantle and I feel so blessed
When the call comes "To Arms", I know that you'll go
Knowing what transpired, at the battle of Taranto

Footnote.....
The brand new Littorio and Vio Veneto and four modernised battleships, Cesare, Duillio, Andrea, Doria and Cavour, were all moored in the harbour.

"Taranto and the night of 11 November 1940 should be remembered forever as having shown once and for all, that in the Fleet Air Arm, the Navy has its most devastating weapon"
Admiral Andrew Cunningham,
Commander-in-Chief Mediterranean Fleet

At Taranto the torpedoes were set to run at 27 knots at a pre-set depth of 33 feet. This was calculated to enable the torpedoes to pass under anti-torpedo netting while still allowing the new Duplex magnetic warheads to 'sense' a warship above and explode while passing beneath, or detonate on contact. Taranto's battleship harbour had an average depth of 49 feet.

She was only the Publican's daughter....
By Lowen Pengoose ©4th June 2020

I fell in love with a Publican's daughter
Her beauty, I saw from afar,
She really was quite attractive..
And her Father....well, he owned a bar!

She was happy and smiley and gorgeous,
Her hair it was soft, blonde and wavy,
What could go wrong? Her Dad owned the pub,
And I was on leave from the Navy!

Handsome and dashing, back in the day,
She'd be hard pushed, to resist all my charms,
She'd remember this day, for many a year,
As this matelot entered his 'Queens Arms'

I pulled out the stops, to woo this fair maid,
Sea stories of wind, steam and sail,
Most of them true, but some I made up,
Coz I still had my eye on free ale

She responded in kind, with tales of her youth,
And then with a great deal of candour,
Proudly told me her Dad, was once in 'The Mob',
Indeed, he was a Lieutenant-Commander

I thought.. "I'll play this cool, what ship was he on?",
Thinking.. "maybe she just wouldn't know",
"I can't remember them all", she mused,
"But there was Leander and Scylla and Arrow"

Having proved her credentials, with this nautical knowledge,
I knew this romance was blessed,
Her Dad, a 'Jack Tar' and now owns a pub,
I was so close to my free pint of 'Best'

The courtship it blossomed and flourished,
As do many, of those tender years,
My future assured, with the loveliest of lasses,
A never ending selection of beers

So came the day, to ask for her hand,
I even went down on one knee,
When she said 'Yes', I thought 'Pint of Best',
And this one is bound to be free

I ordered a round, as we were engaged,
And raised a toast, to 'True Love Found',
Imagine my horror, as father-in-law said,
"Congratulations Son, that'll be fifty pound"

Well, when you're in the Navy, you have to go to sea
And that day, came way too fast,
This would really test our love,
Was it strong enough to last?

Well my father-in-law is a very shrewd man,
"When will you be going to sea?",
I simply replied, "It's my last night ashore
And I'd love a beer for free"

The Publican's daughter and I, soon parted,
The Lieutenant Commander, pondered and mused,
"Do not fret, my sweet, darling girl..
..He never got any free booze"

Remembrance
By Lowen Pengoose ©2020

Remembrance is the word that we use,
when we think of a memory we don't want to lose,
So the act of remembering, and emotions we feel,
keep the memories alive and the feelings so real
Remembering some event, we hold so dear,
Could evoke happiness, or maybe a tear
A two minute silence, where nothing is heard,
demonstrates more power, than the oft spoken word
At 11 o'clock on the most sombre of days,
began a tradition we have set in our ways
To commemorate our fallen, in all theatres of war,
when those guns fell silent, with a deafening roar

Wretched fields in Flanders, where the poppies still grow,
A symbol of remembrance, of the blood that did flow

Rememberence is not limited, to a day, date or time,
nor need be accompanied by those bells that do chime
Choose your own time and place, take time to remember
a hero or loved one, don't wait 'till November
Sometimes the memory, shoots out of the blue
you don't choose the moment, let the memory choose you
When this occurs, as it undoubtably will,
take a few moments, let your memory fill,
Fill your mind with that memory, person, or place,
let the thoughts of that moment just fill the space,
The power of remembrance is secondary to none,
to recognise those heroes and the deeds they have done

And if you see an old fella, not looking quite there, looking forlorn,
with a thousand yard stare, don't rush to judgement......
he was probably there!

Doing his duty for king and country,
think of his mates who he'll never see,
As he remembers, so should we all,
what he remembers, is good men fall,

Not the the old man, that you see today,
but a dashing young hero, who helped save the day,
the man you wanted to be, yourself,
the saviour of our great commonwealth
Since the old wars, have all come and all gone,
the Crimea, the Boer, the bombs of the Somme
Through mankinds stupidity, millions have died
But a billion more tears, men women and children have cried

We should thank him in person, and remember his service,
when he hit that that beach hard, eighteen years old with a purpose

Never forget, the price they paid,
always remember, that memories don't fade
This is our duty, those of us who are free,
to remember those souls, lost o'er land, air and sea
To instill in our children, the need for respect,
and to safeguard their future, in every aspect
They then will remember, with bristling pride,
those who laid down their lives, for our freedoms, who died
I'm not saying that war is wrong or its right,
so no matter how much you believe in your plight
the slaying of innocents, is never right,
for goodness sake, it's just a demonstration of might,

From the wars long ago, to todays peace keeping force
Keeping the world true, and on an even course

The wars they still come, like a plague on this earth
And we keep on fighting for all that we're worth
Wars are all deadly, and fought for a cause,
Battles everlasting never stopping to pause
Vietnam, Bosnia, Aden, Borneo
The headstones bear witness, row after row
For the youngsters today, who don uniform
Are proud to serve, and ready to perform
For they are the future, the defence of our realm
And I'm happy to see them in charge at the helm
In God we must trust, but if a war needs to be won
Trust our Armed Forces, to get the job done

For those Brothers and sisters, who heeded the call,
Standing shoulder to shoulder, I salute you all
(Proud to have served)

Passchendaele
By Lowen Pengoose ©30/10/2020

*Dedicated to Private JH Casey, Royal Fusiliers, G/66029
died 09/10/1917 at Passchendaele
commemorated at Tyne Cot memorial.
Inspired by Royal British Legion Passchendaele 100.
Everyone remembered.*

I never knew you, but I know you
Marching as to war,
You never knew me, nor will you
A hero with them all

I never saw you, but I see you
Marching off to fight
You never saw me, nor will you
Blinded by the light

I never heard you, yet I hear you
Undaunted in your quest
You never heard me , nor will you
Now you're laid to rest

I never loved you, yet I love you
You served your country well
You never loved me, nor will you
You fought and died in hell

I never told you, yet I tell you
How brave and never scared
You never told me, nor will you
Just a boy and Ill prepared

I never gave you, yet I give you
All my respect and thanks
You never gave me, nor will you
The nightmares in the ranks

I never called you, yet I call you
To serve your country, and your king
You never called me, nor will you
You sacrificed everything

I never asked you, yet I ask you
What you thought about the fight
You never asked me, nor will you
How we sleep safe at night?

I never needed you, yet I need you
To let me know all's well
You never needed me, nor will you
But your story I shall tell

I never left you, yet I leave you
In that field in Passchendaele
You never left me, nor will you
Stories far too sad to regale

Par afVbc
By Lowen Pengoose ©2020

We've got Percy's and Crabfats and Jolly Jack Tar,
French Foreign Legion, we're the veterans of Par
To banter and brag, it's what we do best
With like minded souls, we are truly blessed.

Throw in a breakfast and you're onto a winner
It's not SlimmingWorld, you won't get thinner
But you will get richer, not judged by your wealth
But richer in mind, happiness and health

We meet when we're happy, or sad or we're tired
For mental well being, or to be inspired
Or we will just meet to take the Micky
Difficult with MP's, they can be quite tricky

Rockapes are fair game, we all have a go
REME and Signals are too bloody slow
Submariners surface, taking deep breaths
Before they dive to the deepest depths

The medics are caring, kind and sincere
Tending the wounded, not showing fear
Animals are also the military's friend
Loyal to their handler, to the bitter end

'Vires in Varietate' for those that know
'Strength in diversity' armed forces show
For we are all brothers and sisters that's true
Not from blood but the flag that we flew

Signed on the line, all willing to die
For freedom and fortune, reach for the sky
Battle of Britain, Normandy , Somme
The roll of honour goes on and on

At breakfast, first Saturday, every month
To regail our stories, of ladies that lunch
We unload our baggage and have a good moan
Services trained, think 'second home'

We all have our demons we don't like to share,
Our brothers and sisters are there, to care
Armed forces and Veterans Breakfast Club
Here for you all with fantastic grub

Give me your tale of woe and worry
I'll get you a coffee with milk and honey
We're here to listen, help and advise
A shoulder to cry on, wipe the tears from your eyes

You served your country with honour and pride
You took the oath, you would have died
For queen and country we stood tall
For freedom and peace, we answered the call

Our service time is over, but we're not done
The breakfast club has just begun
Help and support is what we do
For forces folk ...and that means YOU!

Brothers and sisters in arms are we
Shoulder to shoulder we stand with thee
First to buy a beer at the pub
We are Par Armed Forces and Veterans breakfast club

In through the Out Door

By Lowen Pengoose ©6th May 2020

*(No poets were harmed during the writing of this poem
Any resemblance to any poet, living or dead is purely coincidental
If you have been affected by any of the issues in this poem,
please seek expert help)*

I've been going 'In' through the 'Out' door
Almost all my life
Never known the meaning of happiness
But totally understand strife
For I know things that others cannot,
Must not, ever know
The darkest thoughts inside my mind
Must not be allowed to grow

The saddest of days, the gladest of days
To me they're one and the same
'Tis hard to know the rules by which
My mind should play this game
To 'soldier' on, it must be done
With a smile upon your face
But it's never quite that easy when
You're right back in 'That Place'

To lighten your load, with a heavy heart
Rise up, when you are down
These simple things are not so easy to do
Try wearing a thorny crown
So if some days I'm not looking my best
And I am asked "Are you okay"?
I'll try and smile, but with a sigh
Reply "Right side of the turf, today"

I've tried to cry, but tears don't come
The anger flows like wine
How come everyone's life is perfect?
EVERONE'S, ...but not mine?
So here I shall sit and ponder
This wretched life of mine
Until I feel I am ready
To go 'In' through the 'Out' door
One final time

Combat Stress - 0800 138 1619
Samaritans - 116 123

How Many Medals
By Lowen Pengoose ©2020

What's for dinner tonight Mum,
Can I go and play?,
Pie and mash and peas, son
And yes - you may

Who's that old man there, Dad,
Can I have some more,
He's a British soldier, son,
No, coz you've had four,

Why's he sleeping there, Nan
Must I go inside?
He's nowhere else to go, lad
The Rules must be applied,

What's that on his chest, Sis,
How many do I need?
They're the medals that he's won, bruv
Depends upon your greed

How did he get injured, Pops
Do I have to do that now?
He's been fighting in the war boy
It's all that I'll allow

Where is the help he needs bro,
Can I lend a hand?
Nowhere to be seen bruv!
I just don't understand!!!!!!!

When's this going to end, Mate?
Should I tell a lie?
This is never right, pal
They were prepared to die

Forces of Nature
By Lowen Pengoose ©2020

I feel I've crawled for a thousand miles
Across a desert land
Just like I did in Afghanistan
With Sore and bleeding hands

I Needed to get to my RV
I needed to get right out
This war isn't making any sense
The fighting is so devout

I can't begin to imagine
How it is going to end
In poverty, or humility
Or maybe we just pretend.

I know someone, who has been there twice,
Or even three times, (and Iraq)
He never speaks ill of the evil he's seen
Or the sadness that he brings back

These boys and girls
who fight for us
Aren't heroes when they enlist
But they will never question
What they've trained for, on their shift

They'll save a life, Not once but twice,
They may take a life........or two
They'll save another, and another
As many as they can do

For these are our Services personnel
Ordinary people you pass in the street,
If you ever knew what they'd done in their lives,
To make sure yours were complete

7 Seas and 5 Oceans
By Lowen Pengoose ©2020

Back in seventy-five, when I signed on the line,
Who knew what was waiting for me?..
A blue suit for sure, and knots so obscure..
..and a wonderful life on the sea

But first things were first, and it could have been worse,
We were taught how to fall in, three deep,
We were told to stand tall, then 'Quick March', was the call,
'Twas gone midnight before we could sleep

It was brutal and harsh
But we learned how to march,
Learnt discipline, pride and respect,
And when we were done, at the end of the watch,
Lash up and stow, when all kit's correct

The instruction was hard, But with scant disregard,
For our welfare, we toiled for hours,
Learning signals and flags, we packed our kit bags,
Nautical knowledge would surely be ours.
We were just boys, playing with our toys,
Like rifles and boats and ropes
From all walks of life, mostly poverty and strife,
We shared all of our dreams and our hopes.

A class leader stepped up, to control us young pups,
Help train us, and make us behave,
They picked on the tall lad, who thought that he'd done bad,
Turned out he was the one who could shave.

Moxham, his name, I remember his shame,
Pleading 'I've never taken charge before'
We agreed he was sound, and would not run aground,
If he did, we would help him ashore

Every morning at six, it was 'On Socks and Nicks'
As Reveille, loudly would play,
We'd rush for a dhobi, still sleepy and dopey,
And in to the Rig of the Day.

To learn Rates and Ranks, and then give thanks,
In whichever church we prayed,
Those with no belief, muster at Gunnery Chief,
Who would teach us more arts of our trade.

We did this for weeks, learning brand new techniques,
Like splicing and making and mending,
Ship recognition, how to earn a commission,
The knowledge became never ending.

Then we saw light in the distance, reward for persistence,
Our training was nearly complete,
boyhood to brotherhood, shoulder to shoulder we stood,
......We were ready to join the Fleet

Desire the Right
FIQQ 1ZZ
51°42'S 57°51'W
By Lowen Pengoose ©13th May 2020

*(Dedicated to my shipmates and all who wear the South Atlantic medal with pride.
But especially those 255 who are on eternal patrol)*

April 2nd was the day
All the papers had to say
At 20 years old.....
..you had better learn to pray

The day before was no joke
I was just a normal bloke
Tomorrow would be.....
..The man in me, that awoke

The next 10 weeks would prove to be
Life changing times upon the Sea
We had to sail.....
..And set them Free

Swiftly, the Lady decreed
Retíraos, or find yourselves besieged
My land and people.....
..Will be retrieved

For I have sent a powerful might
To visit thee in dead of night
You really won't want.....
..To fight THAT fight

A deaf ear, they turned
The offer spurned
There were about to be.....
..Several lessons learned

Who Dares Wins arrived with stealth
To wrestle back the Islands wealth
And restore the land.....
..To perfect health

But not without a woeful cost
As the Steel City was sadly lost
And to the depths.....
..Twenty lives were tossed

The same fate came to several more
Whilst keeping safe all those ashore
Two hundred and fifty five souls.....
..Labelled 'Casualties of War'

City of 3 spires, then fell
Sounding again, that same death knell
Antelope and Ardent adrift.....
..when next, death cast his ugly spell

Jumping jets were jumping high
Then standing still in deep blue sky
Wreaking destruction.....
..with measured eye

14th June when silence reigned
What was lost was now regained
But at a cost.....
..Every man forever pained

The memory of this righteous fight
Empire blue, sea green and white
Restored the Islands.....
..'Desire the Right'

The Name of the Game
By Lowen Pengoose ©2020

I love to play games with my children
We always have so much fun
Their ages are 5 and 7
But neither have ever won

My favourite is 'Snakes and Lions'
Where you slither, wriggle and slide
But when it's your turn, if you throw double six
You stand up and ROAR! with pride

Another good one, is called 'Run, Daddy, Run'
Where you pop the kids in the shower
Then run to the pub and down a pint
As the landlord shouts 'Happy Hour'

As card games go, there's a few they like
But their favourite by far is called 'Snop!'
It's a bit like 'Snap!' But the winner must shout
"My poo-poos always go plip-plop!"

The next game we play is called 'Chicken'
But it's not the one you're thinking
This is the one where you stare at each other
And don't even think about blinking

We also involve the family dog
He's family, on that we agree
This game we call 'Itchy Scratchy'
And you're a winner if you find a flea

I-Spy is a family favourite
My 5 year old could've won
But something beginning with 'Door'
Would always spoil the fun

Monopoly, don't get a mention
Board games are boring as hell
I'll just go and my spear gun
So we can play darts as well

If my kids ever beat me, it's over
It'll never happen, I hope and I pray
If it ever does I won't tell you
But you can buy my kids on e-bay

The Beautiful Game
By Lowen Pengoose ©10th June 2020

Since I was a lad, we were all football mad,
Football, not lessons, did rule.
Always kicking a ball, against the toilet block wall,
At Farnham Grammar School.

After school, in the park, until way after dark,
I'd practice bending free kicks.
From the penalty spot, I'd attempt a chip shot,
Trying to fool the goalkeeper with tricks.

After a while, I developed my style,
With the flair of my hero, George Best.
How to advance? I needed a chance,
And I HAD to excel in that test.

The trial that came, was to play in a game,
They brought me on at half time.
I ran (off the ball), and gave it my all,
My performance was surely sublime?

The success I achieved, was hard to believe,
The House Captain, said I would go far.
A player of note, he kindly wrote
Maybe, a footballing star?

So I had a dream, to play for the team,
I thought were the best in the land.
They played First Division, with expert precision,
My ambition had always been grand.

The team I loved so, continued to show,
Their extensive array of skills.
At home or away, to watch that team play,
Would guarantee you, your afternoon thrills.

May I enquire, as to this team you admire?
Is their style fluent, smooth.....even pretty?
Yes sir, indeed, and it's played at great speed,
The one and only....Manchester City.

To see Colin Bell, casting his spell,
All over the pitch, with ease.
Then make a pass, that is always world class
..and THAT goal is Franny Lee's.

Tony Book at the back, foiling every attack,
That opponents could throw at the boys.
If a shot did get through, Corrigan's hands were like glue
The crowd's response, a cacophony of noise.

Their Golden Age on the centremost stage,
Was sixty-nine to about seventy-five.
Showing great skill and flair, amassing their silverware,
Manchester city really came alive.

Leadership was great, it must have been fate,
In those Mercer and Allison years.
Now we know (that's the story), of this dawning glory,
Absorbing those wonderwall cheers.

As does age increase, so follows my caprice,
To be entertained by watching sport.
Alas and alack, football has quite lost the knack,
And my temper is noticeably short.

It's such a shame, that 'The Beautiful Game'
Now seems fuelled by avarice and greed.
Back in the day, players received minimal pay,
But then they, were a quite different breed.

They'd play for each other, a true band of brothers,
And for the pride of the team.
This group of men, would play to the end,
To achieve their every dream.

Football and me, was not meant to be,
I don't watch it at all, anymore.
But if I'm around and about, I still listen out,
For the Manchester City score!

HOWZAT?!

By Lowen Pengoose ©November 2019

Cricket is such a splendid game, played on the village green
It's also played at the MCG, and any ground in between

The captains are first, to take to the field,
to toss the coin aloft
The winner decides, if he'll bat or he'll bowl,
(he'll use spin if the ground is soft)

The teams assemble, on with the pads,
The bowlers loosen up
Batsmen will practice, many a stroke,
and wish themselves good luck

He takes his mark, and asks for leg, or middle and leg per chance,
Then looks all about, the field that's set, (mid-off seems worth a glance)

He faces up, and readies to strike, the bowler charges in
He lets one go about head high, a bouncer to begin

And so it goes, and runs are scored,
And wickets begin to fall
The bowlers change, from time to time, for that is the captains call

Left arm over, right arm round, a chinaman, or maybe spin
Even a Yorker made the show, And hit the batsman's shin

Up went the shout, HOWZAT? He's out, for this is how it's done
When the ball hits your leg, instead of the stumps, You're out-LBW-Plum!

The umpire agrees, his finger goes up, The long walk back begins
It was always to be, technology decrees, That Hawkeye always wins

The first innings ends, a tidy score reached, three hundred and twelve for eight
Now the captain's resolved, the victory's his, and he sets his field in wait

A forward short leg, and deep extra cover, a silly mid on, (for the catch),
Three slips and a gully, the bowlers are ready, should ensure the result of the match

After many an over, with boundaries and byes, the scoreboard looks very tense
Five overs are left, they're two-eighty-two, it just doesn't make any sense

Now there's one wicket left, and not too much time, to ensure the result of the game
If they stick to the plan, change bowlers again, they'll ensure their cricketing fame

The bowler runs in, helped by the wind, and delivers a perfect length ball,
The batsman reacts, takes a swing, and connects, and that one has gone for a four

The last over is here, the crowd are on edge, we all want to know the score
A single is taken, a boundary scored, after the next ball there's only three more

So, five days of this match, are nearly complete, and the batting team need five to win
A No ball will help, or a wide and a bye, none are easy when playing against spin

No runs off the next, a swing and a miss, but square cuts the last ball for four!
He's over the moon, throws his bat in the air, just to be told - You scored four............
It's a draw!

Princess

By Lowen Pengoose - Revised ©March 2012

If you want to be a Princess
There's things you've got to do
Like wearing pretty dresses
And dancing in glass shoes

You've got to be so pretty
But then you surely are
Brush your hair a thousand times
And wish upon a star

I'd have to climb the tower
Just to win your hand
Rescue you from dragons
In some, far-distant land

I'd love to find a Princess
I'll keep searching far and wide
If I ever find my Princess
I hope she'll be my bride

You've always been a Princess
On this we can agree
Please let me be your handsome Prince
Won't you marry me?

We'll be married at my swamp
Donkey by our side
Beautiful Princess Fiona, forever
My Princess and my bride

Missing Bar Blues
By 'Blind' Lowen Pengoose ©19th June 2020

I woke up this morning,
A blues song playing in my mind,
Yeah! I woke up this morning,
But this blues was a different kind,

Now blues is sent down from heaven,
But my 8-bar blues, well it only had 7!

I got right outta my bed, then,
To find my missing bar,
I jumped right outta my bed, man,
Started searching near and far,

Cos my blues ain't a real blues song,
If it's too short, it's not 8-bars long,

Well I thought I'd go ask BB,
If he'd heard of this before,
Yeah, I thought I'd ask that Blues Boy,
All I needed was one bar more,

My song needed resolution,
One more bar, was the only solution,

The great man sat and pondered,
Thought of all the blues he wrote,
Then the greatest bluesman did utter,
Is it missing a bar, or maybe a note?

I had to reply, a whole bar for sure,
He said well that's easy, just write one bar more!

Well, the genius was enlightening,
BB really is 'The King',
"I'll write you one for free boy,
then your blues will really sing"

I politely refused my hero, right after he had said it,
The truth is that I wanted, to take all of the credit,

After speaking with the legend,
I set about the deadly deed,
I was so enthusiastic,
My one bar, I did exceed,

Would it really matter if I had a couple more?
The trouble is, I'd gone and penned another flippin' four!

Now, what to do with these extras!
I really don't know what to do,
So I thought I'd ask EC, (god himself),
If he could help me through,

If Eric Clapton couldn't sort this mess
My dream of the blues was over, unless...

Inspiration came, the blues spoke to me,
Another form I'd heard all about
It was a risk, but one worth taking
12-bar blues, was worth a shout

Many more bars were added, to my original seven
But when I put them all together, I only had eleven!

Now I got the blues, baby,
'Blind' Lowen, really got it bad,
I mean, I really 'got' the blues today,
So it's made me happy, not so sad

I'll never be a bluesman whilst I am so contented
So I've signed up for the evening class,
to learn how to become tormented

Then I'll play those blues, boy
And I'll play them blues real good,
I'll play them blues, with meaning
Exactly as I should

Cos I've found the missing bar, the one that I had lost
But the blues gotta price, baby, and my happiness was the cost

Now I found a bar in Memphis,
I play my guitar, and drink my booze
Yeah I found 'Blues Hall' in Memphis
Where I play the Missing Bar Blues

Lowen Pengoose Blues
By Lowen Pengoose ©15th April 2020

Woke up this morning,
Duh, didn't I don't?
Fell outta mah bed,
Duh, didn't I do?
Put on mah trousers,
And 'phoned my mate Fred....

Got the Blues, baby
But not the usual ones.....
Got the blues.......honey!
The Lowen Peng-oose Blues

Diddly, diddly diddly dum...de dum, dum

My baby, she gone an' left me
Duh, didn't I don't
She gone away again,
Duh, didn't I do?
She gonna do a fast one
And hook up with my friend

Got the Blues, baby
But not the usual ones.....
Got the blues, baby
The Lowen Peng-oose Blues

Diddly, diddly diddly dum...de dum, dum

My baby, I try and call her
Duh, didn't I don't
Was it something that I said?
Duh, didn't I do?
She never said she loved me
But now she is with Fred

Got the Blues, baby
But not the usual ones.....
Got the blues, baby
The Lowen Peng-oose Blues

Diddly, diddly diddly dum...de dum, dum

Don't get up this morning
Duh, didn't I don't
If you've heard a word I've said
Duh, didn't I do
'Cos if you've ever known someone
I hope his name's not Fred

Got the Blues, baby
But not the usual ones.....
Got the blues, baby
The Lowen Peng-oose Blues

Diddidly, diddidily, diddidily, ...dum.....de
Dah, dah!

Cynical Tentacles

By Lowen Pengoose ©2012

Ev'ry body tryin' 'ard, to get in front of it
Ev'ry body want, a little more than they got
Cynical Boss Man, are tryin' 'ard at everytin'
Tryin' to get me, pay for 'is yacht
Me Boss mun, 'ee is a-'ungry
'Ee want me work for free
cynical tentacle is reachin' out slowly
cynical tentacle is reachin' out for me

Establishment takin' back, All ah me spendin'
Ev'ry body want a little more than they got
Cynical taxman tryin' at ev'rytin'
Tryin' to take back, anytin' dat I bought
Duh tax man he try to levy me
Want me pay a fee
Cynical tentacle is walkin' out slowly
cynical tentacle is reaching out for me

Lovergirls are tryin' to, make future safe for dem
Ev'rybody want a little more than they got
Cynical women are tryin' at everyt'in'
Tryin' to take the whole damn lot
Me woman, she want to marry me
Me want to run and flee
cynical tentacle is reachin' out slowly
cynical tentacle is reachin' out for me

All I wanna do is reggae it away today
I got a little bit more than I want
Miracle reggae band are tryin' at everytin'
Tryin' to dance without any t'ar't(thought)
Me want to sit under the palm tree
Dippin' big toe in de sea
The cynical tentacle is sliding back slowly
The cynical tentacle will never get me!

Any time you want to, come reggae wid me

Handy Things, Gloves

By Lowen Pengoose ©April 2020 *Updated August 2020

Back when the world was a much colder place
We all needed to cover our skin
Clothes were invented so we could keep warm
Some had to be thick, others thin

Hats for the head, shoes for the feet
Inspiration, it came from above
Hands that were cold were never left out
And their covering was known as the glove

They started quite simply, a rag wrapped around
But this hampered their function somewhat
So they designed a pouch, to cover the hand
Tied up and secured with a knot

Then they got clever, and made them from leather,
Because that is particularly strong
But they never did label them, left from the right
So you could always put them on wrong

To avoid this mistake, spaces for fingers were made
And obviously one for the thumb
Thus carefully avoiding putting gloves on wrong hands
Just look at what gloves had become

So now the design had been properley tested
And gloves were selling out fast
There was no more to be done to improve on the glove
........until some idiot asked..

Why not cut the back, right out of the glove
Leather's pricey and goes only so far
A new market would open, we'll be rich overnight
We'll sell these, to the owners of cars

Driving gloves were a hit, but not for too long
'Emporers New Clothes' is the phrase in my mind
The sniggers and abuse that was bandied about
Was quite rude, and not nice, and unkind

Back to the drawing board to redesign gloves
Has anyone any thoughts at all?
A voice from the back shouted "Oh yes I have"
Gloves that will help golfers hit their ball

Well this was a thought, no one had had
Never before had this been done
But don't ask me why, in the fullness of time
Golfers ended up with just one

Now a design of the glove that I'm quite partial to,
Is the fingerless type, they're great
So posties keep warm and keep hold of their post
And Milkies grab pints out the crate

The trouble with these, the fingers poked out
And that fingernails were easily bitten
So they sewed up the tops and fingers together
This was soon to be known as the mitten

The little known fact about numbers of gloves
And some of the tales are tall
Is that two are a pair, but what d'you call four?
Well they're known as…..Four Hand-All's

*In March twenty twenty, came a need for plenty
What do you need? the Government asked
Could it be nurses? or more key workers?
No, what we need is ten thousand masks!

So thanks for the offer, generous as is,
But please don't forget those we love
They need PPE, all they can get, I suggest
A million, Supertouch blue, latex free,
Powdered disposable GLOVES!

Le Chien Noir
By Lowen Pengoose ©28th August 2020

I've been a collector of thoughts my whole life,
A strange thing to do, I'll agree,
I didn't intend to collect or accrue,
My first one, really found me

I was only just born not yet even one,
Whilst lying asleep in my cradle,
Suddenly woken, I looked up to see
A thought lying there on the table,

That was my first, you never forget,
Many more followed soon, I'm not lying,
So easy to find if you shut both your eyes
I found them without even trying

I was still a young man when I had 21,
Vingt-et-un pensées as they're known,
I never set out to seek fortune or fame,
But my thoughts had unceasingly grown

I had so many thoughts, I was on News at Ten
My body of thoughts were famous
Even I didn't know why I started this lark
In fact, I felt quite blameless

So I rounded them up, not easy to do,
but my dogs were specially trained,
The thoughts didn't fight, they seemed quite contrite,
They lay down and were readily tamed

The thoughts and the dogs laid down for the night
So nothing more to be done,
All of my thoughts, too many to count
Were sorted and ordered, bar none.

When I awoke, I knew something was wrong
I saw some thoughts were awry,
Some had gone missing, out of my head
The others were in my mind's eye

So I needed the dogs to sort out my thoughts
To tell me, where did they dwell?
The negative ones in the back of my mind
Down the deepest and darkest well

The tail of the dog now wagging my thoughts
And keeping them all in order
The good ones pushed to the front of my mind
The dark ones given no quarter

These thoughts we all have, can be happy or sad
In fact we have no control
The best we can do is arrange them in line
And keep our dogs on patrol

The dogs are trained to mind our thoughts,
They're really good dogs, by and large,
Be careful to keep them really well fed
Lest the black dog should think he's in charge

Elephants, you say?
By Lowen Pengoose ©April 2020

Why are Elephants grey, you say
Why are elephants grey?
Cos if they were pink, you'd inherentley think
That elephants were gay....
.....By gay I mean a happy chappy,
what else would I mean?
But if for any other reason,
why couldn't they be green?

Would leopards change their spots for lots,
of dots, or maybe not,
Because....if they wanted stars or stripes,
then leopards,they would be, not!
Tigers stripes are nice, and bright,
and run straight up and down
So if they wanted different stripes,
would they go round and round? Like the ..

Giraffes who are tall, and have long legs, and long necks,
Which makes them long for...
They do not care if they have spots,
or stripes or gripes , but they are never wrong......
They stand tall, of course they do
Why would they do no other,,
But to protect, the ones they love
Who would not be the other....

mother who, said NO to you,
The, wolf, nee dog, the mutt, the hound, the pooch
Always mans best friend, who sounds
A little like your best friend, who sends
Their love and friendship which never ends
Until the end of time and space, which will never, ever replace
My love for you, always true, never blue
But an excellent, intelligent, elegant friend of mine,
Which also rhymes, with elephants....
That you say are grey

Life

By Lowen Pengoose ©15th July 2020

(The Arrival)
One moment we're on the inside
The next we're on the out,
Knowing nothing of how this world works,
we undertake to shout

We shout because we're angry
or we're spent or we are fraught
We know not what we're doing, or why,
For we were never taught

But crying ushers comfort,
in many different ways
We're learning to survive this life,
in these frightening early days

(The survival)
Now we subsist with feeding,
and sleep is easier to find
Still shouting when we have to,
but calmer in the mind

We're calm because we're warm and clean
and comfortable at heart
To learn to ask for food and milk,
is certainly an art,

A pattern is constructed,
we no not why or how,
'Tis nature's way or telling us,
just what she will allow

(The mindful)
Years pass by with alacrity,
the learning never ends
We interact with many folk,
we learn to make good friends

Develop a sense of humour,
feelings and a soul
Growing into a perfect form,
is ultimately the goal

The shouting has abated,
replaced with inner peace
Some emotions are still hiding,
but they will never cease

(The Revival)
Life is really a form of art
An art we were never taught
But one we are all made to learn
A fight that must be fought

Some find it easy, others not so
To make their way in life
For those of us who struggle
Words cut us like a knife

But words have many uses
And are used for good and bad
I like when people use happy words
Which stop me feeling sad

(The Finale)
And so it goes, life ebbs and flows
We all have our ups and downs
Time ticks on and we move along
Exhausted..... send in the clowns

Three score and ten or so it is said
A life lived to the full
With give and take, for heavens sake
And a lot of push and pull

When my time comes to pass, I will have no regrets
and nothing left to fear
Having Lived a full and happy life
No need to shed a tear

I Read the News Today
By Lowen Pengoose ©23rd September 2020

(All headlines from BBC News online, barring equal pay for brazilian women soccer which is from skysports.com 3rd September 2020)

Thursday 3rd of September
The Headlines in the paper say
Coronavirus testing is rationed
Mortgage deals plummet today

Aviation is slowly dying
The Government, to blame
Another black man killed in the States
The news all sounds the same

Charlie Gard's parents give birth again
Good news in the papers at last
America to get a vaccine next month
A cynic would say that's too fast

Novichok makes the headlines
Thank god not Salisbury again
Weddings are to be allowed outdoors
Now go celebrate with your friends

Aussies protesting the lockdown
Biden is calling for blood
The weather is not much better
Warnings are issued for floods

Local news is not any better
A30 is closed both ways
Jobs are lost at Eden Project
On this, the saddest of days

In sport there are lots of smiles
Van de Beek has 35 million
Top seed is beaten in US open
Equal pay if you're Brazilian

This is the reason I don't buy a paper
The news is depressing and sad
I dip in online for the headlines
Always wishing that I never had

When your heart is breaking
By Lowen Pengoose ©22nd April 2020

I rise and shine each morning
Place a smile upon my face
I keep it in the bedside drawer
My smile has a special, safe place

This smile is very important to me
I think it gives us hope
Otherwise people are inclined
To sit around and mope

So when you see me smiling
Think of something nice to say
Take my smile right off me
And go make someone's day

Don't fret you've taken my smile off me
And left me without one, and sad
My smile is never ending you know
And YOU smiling would make me so glad

A favour that you can do in return
To help make the world go around
Is to let someone else take that smile off your face
And tell where that smile was found

If everyone did this at least twice a day
Can you imagine the speed it would spread
Then all of the headlines would be happy ones
Telling stories of how fast it sped

It would grow so fast they would have to design
A new measure to record the power
I venture the simplest way to say
Would be the number of "smiles per hour"

So after my day of passing on smiles
I'll keep my smile on my face
Until it is time to go to bed
And put my smile back, in its special safe place

Summer

By Lowen Pengoose ©13th April 2020

Summer comes, but once a year
Some are hot, and Summer's clear
Some are cool, some are wet
What comes this year, we know not yet

Seasons come, and go around
Winter brings a cold, wet ground
Summers hope, will eternal Spring
When we all laugh, and blackbirds sing

Or turn Autumnal, when Summer's over
To look toward, a warm October
Fall from grace, from Summer to Winter
September gales, and trees that splinter

Round and round the seasons go
when nature's dormant, and then she grows
Ever changing mood, she never rests
In my opinion, Summer is the best

As Summer appears, she takes Springs baton
With a request for the sun, to go put his hat on,
The sun may comply, or he may not
But we all hope, this Summer is HOT!

If she doesn't do, what we're hoping for
It matters not, because Summers door
Is opened up, and that in itself
is all we need, to promote good health

Vitamin D, Summer will bring
And Summer will thank, the opening Spring
For bluebells and daffodils, snowdrops, and all,
Spring becomes Summer, this seasons haul

Some are Summers, to remember
Others relegated, to December
Some are Summers we wish to forget

Let's all hope that this one brings
warmth and butterfly nets

The Runner
By Lowen Pengoose ©21st January 2021

I feel I've been running all of my life
From lawmen, gangsters and my latest ex-wife
The taxman I avoid, at every chance
Carefully evading his unwelcome advance

I run from the bankers, I have no interest
In their filthy luchre, a tempting mistress
My contempt for accountants, is way overdue
Counters of money, till their faces are blue

The Police are of course, just doing their job
So I run from the crowds, or the angry mob
Whilst constantly running, ducking and diving
I'm difficult to find, without actually hiding

I run with a plan, so I'll never quit
Like a moving target, I'm difficult to hit
But I'm running to nowhere, I've nowhere to be
Now I'm fated to run; Run constantly

I need a goal, a journey's end
A landing place upon which to descend
It must be somewhere, safe and secure
A destination so placid and pure

A garden of Eden all my own
The safest place that I've ever known
Then perhaps, my running could cease
When I find the meaning of true inner peace

I reached deep inside to search my soul
Identify why I wasn't whole
The answer I found was a simple one
I had just lost the art of having fun!

The persuit of happiness would be my aim
I would run toward this hypnotic flame
Run as fast as I ever had
The goal to be happy and never sad

It really was easy, I didn't even try
Recalibrate the mind, find a natural high
Now in a 'Happy Place' : A Joy to be
But unless I keep running I never feel free

I thought running was the problem, how wrong could I be
I was running from life, trying to flee
Now that I'm running to a place I decide
I'm happy to run with you by my side

Sleep

By Lowen Pengoose ©February 2020

Sleep, sleep, where art though
Why do I lie awake?
I've been lying here for at least three hours
Let me sleep, for goodness sake

I felt so tired after a busy day
I wanted to sleep for hours
But when head hit pillow
I started to think, of the garden, the borders, the flowers

Sleep, sleep I need you now
Why do you just desert me
I've thought of you, the whole day through
Why do you always thwart me

Sleep, sleep, I know you not
I'll never know your peace
Damned to the eternal wake
My sleeplessness will never cease

One day I know I'll sleep again
I'll sleep for evermore
I don't wan't that day to come so soon
I love this life much more

The Drifter
By Lowen Pengoose ©7th January 2021

I drift into another world
A mix of love and fear
Not holding back a better life
But holding back a tear
Hope, forever hopeful
I need the perfect life
My thoughts forever thoughtful
Always cut me like a knife

Should I come, or should I go
I never can decide
Which path will I ever choose
Who will be my guide?
To be the person I've become
Who have I left behind?
Forever me and no one else
Have I become so blind?

So onward friend, and upward
To discover more of me
Walk with me along this path,
This path of discovery
For if we do not try to change
We just stay the same
And that my friend is never good
That is not the aim

I believe we must improve
In every way we can
To make our lives mean something,
To be a better man
Always kind and helpful
Especially when you're low,
Will make you feel uplifted
Then you will surely know

Happiness is contagious
It will aways make you smile
With that smile upon your face
You'll go the extra mile
My advice to one and all
Do not a Drifter be
Choose a path and see it through
Your heart will fill with glee

In these troubled times today
People need our aid
Will you make a difference?
Will you make the grade?
No need to be a superhero
Just be the best you can
Make a difference every day
That is the Master Plan

Always lead by example
People follow in your ways
So drift no more, my wayward friends
We're heading for better days
Now my drifting days are over
I have vision and a goal
It's taken a life of drifting, but
I have truly cleansed my soul

Internal Combustion Abstention
By Lowen Pengoose ©31st May 2020

Alone in a crowded room, full of family and friends,
The love is overpowering it keeps coming, it never ends

Overcrowded in this lonely room, lots of time to think,
Loaded up with luv'n'hugs, they can't see I'm about to sink

Yes, I'm fine, how are you? Do you need a favour?
He's alright, why do you ask?, he will never waiver

Soldier on, stiff upper lip, there's no need to question,
Of course he's okay, don't be absurd
I sneer at your suggestion

He's my rock and my great oak tree
What are you implying?
Of course he's happy, they're tears of laughter,
Don't be silly, why do you think he was crying?

He doesn't cry he has no need,
Why would he waste his time?
My man's a rock, a giant, a god
No need o'tears, that man of mine

Yet in this overcrowded room, I gently sit and weep
No one knows, or cares, or shares
The troubles I have, so deep

On the outside all is good, nothing troubles me
But look into my heart and soul,
You'll see another me.

When you meet this man, you will realise
It is me, just the same
A slightly different view of life
Same man, same face, same name

But inside here, the thoughts run around,
I try so hard to tame them,
If they did out, unchecked by me,
It would result in a riot, and mayhem

So here I sit in this crowded room,
Just me and my million thoughts
Being polite and smiling a lot
But my nerves all jangled and taut

Good old me, I've rallied on
Another day, done and dusted,
Off to bed and press 'reset'
Another day internally combusted!

Makes No Sense
By Lowen Pengoose ©1st July 2020

When you look deeply at this, what sight do you really see?
I see beauty, art, and science, as clearly as can be

When you listen intently at this, what sound do you really hear?
I hear sorrow, love and longing, I hear it loud and clear,

When you breath in slowly at this, what scent do you really smell?
I smell history, life and nostalgia, stories only time can tell

When you touch gently on this, what emotion do you really feel?
I feel happiness, pride and excitement, helping me to heal

When you drink in greatly at this, what flavour do you taste?
I taste sweetness, honey and nectar, delights too good to waste

Our senses are our perception
Sorting truth from deception
Our senses are a guardian angel
Saving us from all things painful

Friends

By Lowen Pengoose ©Decemebr 2019

Feeling strong today, now
Feeling strong today
I'll help you feel empowered
Together, let us pray

Have you lost your way, now
Have you lost your way
Let me help you back on track
Right Here, you must NOT stay

Feeling rather tired now
Feeling rather tired
Why not linger just a while
A short rest is required

Are you in pain, now
Are you really in pain
I'll come and take your hurt away
To make a stronger chain

Can't do this alone now
Can't do this alone
Together we are stronger
This I've always known

Will it ever end now
Will it ever end
It seems everlasting
I could really use a friend

Here we go again, now
Here we go again
Put a brave face on it
We must be near the end

This noise is very loud, now
The noise is very loud
The voice inside is shouting
Being heard is not allowed

But I can't complain, now
I will not complain
I have my health and many friends
To take away my pain

Good Grief

By Lowen Pengoose ©2020
(In memory of my mother Brenda Mary Pogson 25/3/1932 - 12/3/1998)

Ghosts are neither real or unreal,
They exist in the mind to help people heal,
To heal from the loss of loved one, or friend,
To help both the heart and mind try to mend.

Ghosts do not haunt or spook or scare
The spirit form exists, to allow you to care
Your loved ones form will still remain
For a period of time to sooth your brain

For the loss of one, so dear to you
Instils more grief than you ever knew
The spirit remains for a period of time
Coaxing your body back to its prime

When your mind, is healthy and fit
And grief is climbing out of the pit
Your despair is less than yesterday
And tomorrow may be the day you pray

There will come a time, only you know when
You can face rejoining the world again
That's when the ghosts will disappear
Into loving memories for you to hold dear

The rest of your life forever changed
Without your permission, rearranged
Your loved one forever out of sight
Yet with you morning, noon and night

In My Time of Dying
By Lowen Pengoose ©11th February 2021

I lie wounded upon this battlefield
Awaiting my final breath
A million lucid memories I see,
In that infinite split-second before death

Surprisingly I feel no pain or panic
Only calmness and serenity
These beautiful images fill my mind
Rejoicing in my identity

This calmness completely envelopes me
Cleansing, warm and pure
I examine each and every thought
Regardless how obscure

I look to the West, where the sun sets
Only to see my sweet wife, and my mother
Both loving and caring, and weeping for me
Trying to comfort and console each other

Battle smells of cordite hang ominously
Pungent, acrid, almost dry
Is it that scent or the memories
Exacting a tear from my eye?

These thoughts and memories arrived as one
But each hold equal measure
As I view them simultaneously
I notice no pain, only pleasure

My next evocation surprises me
A remembrance of a childhood past
My first day of school, the happiest of times
The day the die was cast

These numerous memories stand together
Reminders of a life ever present
I stand on the threshold of eternity
Making ready for my concluding ascent

I can no longer discern the sounds of battle
No mortars, rockets or shells
A beautiful quietude descends all around
Save the pealing of heavenly bells

These myriad images depicting my life
All remain in sharp focus within me
Not flashing past as we are led to believe
While proving the truth really does set you free

Yet in that instant 'twixt life and death
Assuredly, the shortest to exist
Is also the most prolonged moment in time
As if it were your very first kiss

I see every face of all those I have loved
Omnipresent with happiness and cheer
My children's laughter 'gainst the peal of the bells
All I've dreamt of so gratefully near

No regrets have I in my last moment on earth
My final reckoning at hand
If you're true to yourself, above all else
You hold the key to the promised land

My body has long since been interred
Three score and ten years plus a few
The memories and visions still as vivid within
Remain bright and sharp with colours anew

Nirvana, the destination we all seek
Is not found on earth, I'm not lying
The million memories you will see for evermore
Will be in your time of dying

Any Questions?

By Lowen Pengoose ©November 2019

To be, or not to be.....
Is of course the question,
To be kind, or not to mind,
You choose your direction.

To be fair, or not to care,
Which one do you favour?
Should you be true, or change your view
Be careful not to waver

Do you take, or do you give
Which side do you stand
For if in need, no sign of greed
Why not a helping hand?

To step forward or step back
You always have the option
You steer your craft ahead, abaft
For you sir, are the coxswain.

Do you come or do you go
How do you decide
But twists and turns are how one learns
To put your doubts aside

Once clear in mind and pure of thought
You choose your direction
With hopes and fears and salty tears
And love as your protection

So when you ask for my advice
Well this is my suggestion
To be, or not to be.....
Is indeed THE question

Printed in Great Britain
by Amazon